BONE MUSIC

BONE MUSIC

poems by
Joel Peckham

STEPHEN F. AUSTIN STATE UNIVERSITY PRESS

Production Manager: Kimberly Verhines
Book Design: Jerri Bourrous

IBSN: 978-1-62288-912-9

For more information:
Stephen F. Austin State University Press
P.O. Box 13007 SFA Station
Nacogdoches, Texas 75962
sfapress@sfasu.edu
www.sfasu.edu/sfapress
936-468-1078

Distributed by Texas A&M University Press Consortium
www.tamupress.com

Contents

Acknowledgements . . . 7

Prologue . . . 9

I. *The Quantum Soul*
The Wreckage that We Travel In . . . 13
Astrocartography . . . 19
A Cheap Hotel In Aqaba . . . 21
Any Moonwalker Can Tell You . . . 23
Alien Technology . . . 24
All that Is Holy . . . 25
Fire in the Cockpit . . . 27
To the Woman I Backed Into At The Kroger Parking Lot . . . 29
Glaciations: Notes on the Last Ice-Age . . . 32
The Quantum Soul . . . 36
Re: Like a Box . . . 38
Any Moonwalker Can Tell You, II . . . 40
Preoccupied at a Café in Portland, Maine . . . 42
Going Sideways . . . 43

II. *In Case of Emergency*
Arrhythmia . . . 49
Field Sobriety . . . 57
A Word Misheard . . . 59
New and Bitter Flowers . . . 60
Witness . . . 62
RE: Wisdom . . . 63
In Case of Emergency . . . 64
Sewers . . . 66

Suffering Tape . . . 69

The Tongue is a Fire . . . 71

What It Means To Drift . . . 73

Bone Music . . . 75

The Locomotive of the Lord . . . 77

Acknowledgments

There are too many people to whom I am indebted and without whom this book would not exist. First I should acknowledge the feedback and support I received each step along the way from Rachael Peckham and Darius Atefat-Peckham—incredible writers and readers as well as the great loves of my life. Special thanks also to Robert Vivian, Wendy Barker, Laura Michelle Deiner, Jeff Tigchelaar, Daniel Lasselle, Nicole Lawrence, Ryan Faulkner, Kayla Queen Dyer, Tony Viola, Eric Smith, Michele Schiavone, Mary Moore, Marie Manilla, S. Diane Wellman, Craig Challender, Art Stringer, Marc Harshman, Kevin Carollo, Nayt Lundquist, Travis Dolence, Lily Jurskis, and John Van Kirk who all read and gave feedback on early versions of these poems. With love to my family, especially Joel Peckham Sr., Jeanne Peckham, Tina Kemp, and Lisa Maidment. Love as well to all those I have played music with, especially Reuben Ambat, Eric Jonsson, Davis McGraw, John Salvage, Julia Grimmet, Stephanie Fernandes, Andy Ambat, D.T., Reid Moak, Miles Sheft, Boscoe Sheff, Jared Allen, David Slitsky, and Drew Maidment. Eternal gratitude to Sara Henning, Kimberly Verhines, and the entire staff at SFAP for the work they have done on this manuscript. And thanks always to Robert Pack, who started me on this path so many years ago.

Grateful acknowledgement is also given to the magazines and anthologies where many of these poems were originally printed, sometimes in slightly different forms:

Cave Wall: "RE: Like a Box," "All That is Holy," and "Glaciations: Notes
    from the Last Ice-Age"
Cloudbank: "The Wreckage that We Travel In" and "Fire in the Cockpit"
The Cold Mountain Review: "RE: Wisdom"
The Free State Review: "Field Sobriety"
Grist: "A Cheap Hotel in Aqaba"

Jelly Bucket: "Witness," "In Case of Emergency," and "Going Sideways"

The MacGuffin: "Prologue" (Originally published as "Arrhythmia I")

Mud Season: "The Tongue is a Fire," "Preoccupied at a Café in Portland, Maine" (originally published as "Preoccupied"), and "What it Means to Drift"

Nimrod: "Sewers 1, 2, and 3" and "The Locomotive of the Lord"

The Southern Review: "Astrocartography" and "Alien Technology"

Spillway: "Suffering Tape"

Subprimal Poetry and Art: "Among the Tunnels"

The Sugar House Review: "The Quantum Soul"

Tar River Poetry: "Any Moonwalker Can Tell You"

Tiferet: "New and Bitter Flowers"

The Tishman Review: "A Word Misheard"

On Unity: Coming Together, Falling Apart: "Arrhythmia 1-8"

Prologue

—on listening to Charlie Parker's alto break in Gillespie's "Night in Tunisia"

Rhythm

suggests eternity. But there are so many rhythms. And we are nearly
    always
comping, vamping, layering one upon another. Dropping bombs
on the solo like Roy Porter on the skins, coming in—
off. Breaking apart

the beat only to stop. Leaving the Bird gliding in space— so high
and alone that it wasn't "Night in Tunisia" anymore—or any song, any
    place or time but everywhere
and always. With his own idea of what the pattern
wasn't, with the joy and terror of building and

breaking. Waiting. Wondering where the next beat would come, if it
    would come. And the sense that yes, it would
come, a pulse, a roll to bring him back into the song completely new
if he didn't just play but listened

and was lost.

I. The Quantum Soul

The Wreckage That We Travel In

Cathy: What will happen to us, in time?
Bullitt: Time starts now.

1.

The world must take us by surprise—in spite of all the warnings, all the evidence. Even a man whose life is shaped by loss takes each new blow in bafflement. So when the Corolla died after 294,000 miles and my son held a black garbage bag open as I scrambled, sweating, to clean out the cab before the wrecker came, I couldn't quite believe it—tossing in old CDs, cassette tapes in the wet heat and haze of the alley behind the Autotech, thinking of the many states we rolled though—the places we lived in, left unscarred, unscathed without so much as a scratch or a dent—thinking of how much of our lives we spent trying to get from one place to another, fugitives with nowhere to go and no one to chase us—idling in traffic on the Garden State, or climbing the hills of Maryland, cresting as eighteen wheelers shuddered up behind as if tossing out a line to reel us in, pulling us back, to be shot out again, touch and go as we plowed through snow and rain and up into clouds to be thrown down into valleys of Morgantown and Charleston. Melted crayons on the back seat, tufts of fur floating up from a long dead golden retriever. Memory—

a space we build as we enter it and in entering, change. *Is there anything still here of him, of them?*—a nickel that slipped between the cushions of a seat, a hairpin, the stick of a lollipop that traveled more than a decade, through time and heat. *Anything worth keeping?* Of the son and wife I'd lost in another car on another continent, on the other side of the world. Somewhere, all the pistons fire, growling. I think of Steve McQueen stealing the body from the morgue, and roaring through the streets of Russian Hill, first chased then chasing, held to earth only a little by gravity and speed as if one could cheat the news of death simply by jumping in a car and driving. We tried and for a while it seemed to work. But you can't just keep on running. Time catches the bullet in its teeth each time, and each time we look on in disbelief.

2.

There was the old Ford Escort Wagon that came to rest in the abandoned lot in Milledgeville behind the auto dealership and those drives out of Michigan into Canada north of the lakes across the grey winter tall grass of Ontario as the boys watched the Wizard of Oz and Willy Wonka and Chitty Chitty Bang Bang on a small TV set Susan rigged to rest between the seats—one boy singing off key, the other hooting, humming, inarticulate as we crossed over Niagara's rushing waters down to northern Maine and how, in a honeymooner hotel I tucked them beneath pink sheets as Cyrus cried about the strange man in the purple coat in the boat with lights all around it and the woman with the green skin and the man who lured children with candy into a cage on wheels. And I remember telling him he was safe and I would keep him safe, that a movie was like a dream you could wake from. Or like the memory of a dream. *It can't hurt you, honey. Not really.*

The lies we tell our children we tell ourselves

to protect ourselves, I think.

3.

And the Buick Skyhawk I murdered that spring when I was 19 when
the head cover gasket blew on 95 on a Sunday afternoon just outside of
Litchfield on the way back to college after my cousin's wedding. How
I stood on the side of the road with miles ahead and behind and no
idea where to go or what to do. Steam coming off everything, shifting
light and air and pavement. Afraid to flag down help, afraid to begin the
long walk in painful shoes up or down the interstate, the tarry current
tugging at my tie as I waited for a miracle. It came (I forget his name), a
retired mechanic in a dirty white t-shirt that hugged his belly so it slung
low in front of him like a net heavy with fish. He chained the front axle
to his truck and I steered behind him off the highway past farms and
into woods, away from the tidal roar of the road, away from everything,
thinking of every B-grade horror movie I'd ever seen as we turned and
turned again, dust billowing, floating into sunlight and shadow of tunnels
thick with leaves. Nice man. Poured me coffee in a tidy little kitchen at a
Formica table with little minnows stenciled all along the edge and let me
call my father from his phone as he worked the car for three hours, trying
to seal cracks that spidered through steel like veins in a leaf, like fractures
in bone. *But they was too many* he said. *They was everywheah. Might go a hundred.
Might not. Might get you home. Might could. I think it will. Maybe. But aftah that
. . .* He lifted his shirt to wipe the sweat from his chin. I looked away and
down, studying patterns of little fish swimming through seaweed. *No.
No. Son. It's ok. Don't blame yahself,* he said. *Nothin' lasts and really, what can
you do? It's a Buick.*

4.

Would it be better to cease remembering or like my father slowly have it fall away in pieces, petals floating off, growing heavy with water until they sink past reach. This life, these things that we accumulate and carry—these engines in the cages they keep rattling, the purr of combustion all the explosions firing so fast they've lost distinction—blur and blend into one thing—violence so regular it soothes us to an almost sleep past caring knowing but not touching or touching all around like water warmed to body heat—what is a day a life a body—what is a window a windshield a world beyond—a matter of perspective and a sheet of glass all that separates the one from the many, this life from the next—what could send us crashing, flying into it? As a boy hurtling

up 93 with my father to visit his father in the nursing home, I loved to stare directly at the trees until they blurred and I could feel that killing speed and imagine I was me and not me and me and the car fell away, a dropped shield as I soared and tumbled. Sometimes I remember, further out in winter, boys would skate past safety. Somehow

holding themselves together by being far away, framed by the window. Gliding on glass like planes descending toward Logan, lifting off from Providence. Solitary. Separate. Free.

5.

How do you let go an emptiness, an ache? Slit the net? Catch and release?
Do you fill it like a cup or pour it out like water into water? A man wet to
the knees, taking a shovel to the sea.

For years I've carried them with me at the corners of my eyes or just
outside the frame of the rearview in the backseat singing in and out of
tune

off time, off key. And even if I were to forget everything. Even their
names. Even my own name which would be to forget the name of my
father as his father forgot his name finally. I have to believe

I would still hear them feel them—passengers beside and behind. And
maybe, like my father's father, in time, I will mistake one name for
another, as one road becomes another, one space flowing into space,
one leaf to the greater green. I'd like to think there is an end to running
where all things come together in a stream. Maybe it is that simple. That
easy. When your grip has been so tight your palm is stinging red and you
know it

is time, past time to unclench the hand, and with all the reverence of one
abandoned in abandoning his faith, grow tired of the chase, hand over
the keys.

Astrocartography

1.

When I was ten I won a contest with a friend for holding my breath
        underwater. It was a dare and I hated him for that, hated them,
        boys naked and shivering in the sun, pointing from the floating
        dock. Laughing. How they knew how much I feared the water
        and the dark. That pressure in the lungs and how the cold stung
        my eyes wide in the murk. After he exhaled, exploding

up and out, I stayed down there for another 10 seconds just to make
        them worry, just to make a point. Then swam up lazy, slow,
        drifting as globes of light spun and streamed from my mouth
        and nose. For the rest of the day I saw stars floating on the
        periphery

of my vision. Sometimes

I still do.

2.

Like most I have survived things no one should. But here we are, aren't
        we? Miracle of miracles. With another surgical scar, another
        loss, another lesson that doesn't apply to any other situation and
        brains starved for oxygen. I am trying

to believe that pressure and loss can focus the mind, or like thesaints in a
        fire, bring visions. Did they hold their breath as the smoke rose
        up or did they welcome the heat into their lungs hoping to see
        God? It is terrifying

to drown and terrifying to live and terrifying how quickly we adapt,
pulling ourselves onto the dock as if nothing had happened,
leaving a world behind only to realize much later that parts of us
are changed or gone. And so

I can't let go even as I stare down at my empty hands, swimming toward
the bottom. I do not know what I hope to find. A single shoe
unlaced, the skeletons of fish, a sippy cup, a teddy bear, a reason.
Searching out what's missing? Diving into that tear

in the cosmos? Trying to recreate an ancient map of stars to guide us home.

A Cheap Hotel in Aqaba, 2/6/2004

Over a tea-stained sink I gather memory, cool water in cupped hands and
    dip my face to put out the sun
in my cheeks and forehead and back of the neck and maybe some shame
    in the way that Susan would lick a thumb
and finger to pinch the wick and turn a flame to a wavering ribbon that
    snakes
toward evening all along the avenue, Al Hussein Bin Ali. In the cheap
    hotel in Aqaba the air is thick
with cardamom and lamb, dripping from a thousand spits in a thousand
    shops that rattle through the souk with shouts and laughter bright as
    shanti bells. The unit in the window tilts
dangerous, and hums a cool damp pulse.
Sand is in our hair, our socks, our underwear, the lining of our coats. The
    boys already drift off in their cots, dreaming of stone the color of
    pale roses as they float and spin as if still
on the surface of water heavy with salt, miles to the north. And I can
    almost hear
Susan with her mother across the hall in another 15-dollar room. And
    I want
and do not want to know what they are talking about. It is not yet dark
    but drifting
in that direction and the women in their hijabs hold each other's hands as
    they walk into water to their knees, fully clothed. Somewhere
a man is heading out for another night's work in an old truck. He
    crouches, checks the sweepers, bangs a long pole on the
    undercarriage to shake off clumps of dirt. Coughs, lights one of a
    thousand cigarettes smoked down to the filters or unfiltered, to the
    lips. Tonight
the highway of the Kings is clean and clear of sand

and accidents and ghosts of prophets traveling. Tonight
we sleep apart in separate rooms. Tonight
we long for something which seems far off as the memory of the scent
    of smoke or steam somewhere in a city that does nothing but call us
    to windows we can't see out of or beyond, any more
than we can see through dreams of children or lovers on their last night
    together and apart. (I wish
I could remember, how we came undone. But
I can only say that it was like
watching an accident happen from a mile away or sleeping through it
    in the backseat as the night goes tumbling. Slow and fast at once and
    terrible)—
a matter of one being near the end of things and the other, not yet
    beginning and with no way of catching up. (My son and I will spend
the rest of our lives chasing that ribbon down that busy street). Tonight
the cheap hotels of Aqaba all hum and lean toward
the city which leans toward
the sea, listening.

Any Moonwalker Can Tell You

It has a smell, a scent—floating in on solar winds, star-sputtering from
    surfaces of stone, following you back
to the module, clinging to suits, to boots and bags. Born of meteors, and
    lava flows, sour with spent
cartridges and the barrels of guns. How a breath could tear apart the
    lungs, unzip the chromosomes,
how dust clung to everything, charged,

airborne. Back at mission control, in a haze of smoke, engineers and
    scientists smiled, nervous, laughed, lost
in a whirring clatter as equations kept on truing up—the craft did not
    sink into the powder, and the powder
carted back to a capsule full of oxygen did not smolder, burn, explode
like a star. Deep breaths all around. Easy to miss
a tickle in the back of the throat, a persistent

cough. What kills is never what we plan for. You have to look so close to
    see when change comes slow, and there's so much to blind us. After all,
on the bright side where there is no dusk, we are all
moonshot and shining on the sea of tranquility and the ocean of storms
    under a clear sky, black
as basalt, struck like matches, floating

like dust.

Alien Technology

Sometimes I want to take it all down to the studs, the way a kid on my block once took apart his deadbeat father's motorcycle (he'd been gone almost a month), using a ratchet set and tools found in the garage, sure he could put it back together exactly right if he placed each bolt, each nut, frame and fork, in a line on a blanket in the order in which it was unscrewed, and then worked backward. *Reverse Engineering*, he told us. *This is what they do with the saucers they capture*, and we watched him grunt and sweat, covering his t-shirt and his jeans with grease, before we left him one by one, pedaling home before the sun had passed below the treeline.

Yesterday I heard an explosion, saw a sunburst flash into the darkness and then the lights on all the houses on our street went out at once. Later we would learn how a semi too big for the back-road along the highway had clipped an electrical wire and just kept going as everything stretched and popped, trailing and writhing behind in a shower of sparks. In memory

I move the scene back and forth, like a DJ in a dark club scratching a record in the middle of a song, the world astutter, askip. To find the moment there is no returning from and turn it like a dial, or at least to see it as it comes, if it comes—to reproduce the solo as it was on the original recording, note for note. But we don't know by knowing. As if

in making love we could retrace our steps and bring the body to climax again and again as if it were all one body arcing to the tongue and worked the same way every time. Where would be the darkness and the sparks? We go and keep on going. And even if we could get that engine to restart, where are all the flying saucers? Tell me that? They should be everywhere.

Unless they are.

All That is Holy

For the love of all that is holy, why? He'd shout, hammering a fist on the dash,
  staring over the roofs of cars, craning his head out the window in a
  futile attempt to see around the flatbed towing the doublewide into
  a one-lane merge on 93 just outside of Fitchburg at 5pm. *Jesus Christ,
  God*

Damn it to hell. My father who was and is forever in a hurry—even when
  he has nowhere to go and the off-ramp is already far too close. The
  man who arrived at his mother's wake an hour before the parlor had
  unlocked the doors so we had to sit in the car listening to Elvis as
  the windshield fogged away the city of Medford. If you're not 15
  minutes early, he'd tell me, handing me a bucket of balls on the way
  to the field before anyone else had even gotten to the locker-room,
  you're 30 minutes late. And so I was and still I find myself

more often than not, shagging my own fly balls in an empty outfield, or
  counting minutes, seconds, sometimes sweating or saying a prayer as
  I watch the clock. Like a rigged explosion in a mineshaft, life as lit
  fuse. Come on . . . Come on . . . . Do you start running or stomp it
  out? Or try to keep your eyes open as the powder ignites and the air
  becomes a pressure wave alive with shrapnel? And who isn't a little
  afraid

of such ravishment, tearing by us, through us past the speed of sound?
  All that superheats the lungs. All that hits us all at once. The bullet
  strikes before we hear the shot. For the little boy at the bottom of the
  pool desperate for oxygen but holding his breath not wanting to lose
  the magic of the blue world he has entered. And the couple holding
  hands in the waiting room of the cancer treatment center. For

everyone anxious to get on with it and afraid of it coming, waiting for a
chance to speak while wishing for silence, starting up the car before
we have our seat belts on. Lord, how can I learn to slow it down, to
touch and hold each moment of this life, taking joy in making time,
bending it to rhythm as hands flutter like moth wings down the back
to the base of the spine. So I am always

swinging a bucket of balls as I walk loose-limbed with my father just
before the start of summer and after the last bell has rung, or
watching Rachael brushing off the beads of water after a bath,
envying the towel.

Or sitting in traffic as I do now, the perfect light of evening shimmering
every burning hood and windshield

and all their colors flashing and shaking in the haze of summer into one
sinuous animal as it glides over smooth tar. For

the thwack and smack of wood on leather. For the blue sky that holds
us for a moment at the apex of its arc. For all that we have missed
while waiting to merge, not knowing how or why but only that this
too, all this

must be holy.

Fire in the Cockpit

—Gus Grissom

We are all in space,
all the time she says, holding the hand of her wide-eyed son as they walk
    through the air
and space museum and I think of SETI and Solo and Kirk and Apollo
1 and 13 and the shuttle the earth would not set free and the one that broke
apart upon reentry. No wonder we long for some
swashbuckling captain to steer us through the asteroids on bravado and
    bluster, convinced of his own cleverness and unafraid. I think

of late winter nights, snow flurries whirling in the dark outside my frosted
    windows, and sneaking down to my father's den to watch, nose to
    screen, green skinned girls dance
and alien folk musicians sing and how, from my little capsule of a room
    in the split level ranch on the gravel road behind the Kmart off of
    Main Street, I dreamed
of a universe that warm, familiar, full of life, that could be
travelled at warp speed, light speed, stars lengthening and streaming on
    either side so I might be

slung somehow unharmed across the great expanse of many galaxies.
    The Earth swings
around the Sun, a child spun in a circle at the end of his mother's hands,
    his feet raised off the ground and the Sun is whipped
around center of the galaxy, and the Milky Way itself has let go, come
    free-falling, flying and its all hurtling
through something, somewhere, like a car in stealth mode driven by
    some kid, hormone-high and whooping down an unlit street—lights
    off, windows down. It should be

enough the way we surf the hood, stars threading through our fingers.
   Must we always be, pushing at the edges, trying to escape this world
   for another even as it takes us
pinballing away with the force of gravity and entropy and all the time
the heat is rising and there is nowhere to go, as everything begins to
   tremble and shake, lights flashing. Oh captain, what
was the last thing that you said before the flames filled the module,
   superheating the air? *We've got a fire in the cockpit. Get us*
out of here.

To the Woman I Backed Into at the Kroger Parking Lot

Well, I backed into your *car*. Or actually, your fender. Leaving a ding, a dent, a scratch, a smudge, and you

turning around and around in the busy lot, your door wide open, hands flying up to the air like a couple of birds caught in a window-box. Or maybe you backed into me, or we struck each other, pulling out of our respective spaces at the same time but headed from opposite rows and in opposite directions and so met at the middle at once in a crunch which sounds

unlikely but then so is existence. None of this had to happen, none of it intentional–the planet, the atmosphere made from all those random comet strikes, me, you, Rachael, the internal combustion engine, etc., unless you believe there was a plan and if even if there was, it was not mine. Even as a writer I would not have, for example, included the bit about both cars being the same model and make but different years. Two Subaru Outbacks colliding in the night. Well, in the early evening, in a parking lot in West Virginia. I swear

I looked in my rearview and my side-view and over my shoulder and you weren't there. And I'd bet you did the same and I was not there either. Until you were. I was. And there we were. We are. I swear

it didn't feel as if I'd hit a thing that was already stopped. I've delivered hits before and been hit and this felt more like a bouncing off than a driving into. But I admit I was distracted and tired and it was 5pm and I was looking into the sun and had taken off my glasses because of the glare. So I don't know. I said *what are we looking at* which was stupid. Maybe if I had said *I'm sorry* or *are you O.K.?* things would have gone better for both of us, but I could already see the damage wasn't much and you seemed unharmed if spitting mad and I was still a little shaky and unsure I was at fault. I'm still not sure, though I'd like to think I would have offered to pay for damages.

I didn't, I said, *what are we looking at* and when you pointed at your fender I said, *Ok. What do you want to do?* thinking, we could talk this out, come to some arrangement that wouldn't make my premiums go up. The damage was minor. No one was hurt. Accidents happen all the time. But

you wanted our insurance card and so I looked at Rachael who by now was standing next to both of us and looking a little sick herself (this was *her* car, not mine) and she went back to the car to dig it from glove-box. Ok. Fine. That is, of course, your right. And I was about to ask for yours too when you snatched the card from her hands as if she weren't already holding it out in offering

and Rachael asked *why are you so angry* and you said, *I got backed into!* as if you *were* your car and I said, *Ma'am, I think we backed into each other* which was what I thought but maybe not the thing to say right then and you said, voice rising, *No. I had already backed out. You hit me and you're going to pay for it* which of course was not Rachael's point at all, which was in fact, besides the point. She meant only that

no one was hurt, and the damage was slight. Accidents happen. Why couldn't we be decent to each other, even grateful? Which only made us both flustered. Me, ashamed for making things worse and you staring at her as if she'd lost her mind. *I got backed into!* you said again as if everyone around us, carting their groceries and screaming children, cases of beer beneath their arms, were witnesses and jury. As if we were both deaf *and* dumb. *I got backed into!* And even now I wonder how you saw me then.

What kind of man in what kind of story. Which makes me wonder how many times you'd not been seen and been run into only to have some ass-hole try to tell you it was all your fault for being in his way. And so you took

the insurance card and got in your car, saying *You'll be hearing from me!* and slammed the door, driving off with that card still clutched between your hand and the wheel, leaving

the two of us standing there in the parking lot as if we'd just been struck by something we didn't see coming, a comet flying in from out of no-where, or maybe we were the comet, or were riding it (so much is a matter of perspective) and I'm still looking backward trying to see what I missed and what I didn't, my own eyes in the mirror, looking for yours.

Glaciations: Notes From the Last Ice Age

To Rachael

In the end it's all about the heat:
radiation, convection, conduction. You shivering beneath cool sheets,
    slipping icy fingers
underneath my t-shirt and traveling up my chest or down
into the waistband of my boxer-briefs. Seeking out the warmest places,
    the privates spaces in the hollows of the groin or the armpits or
    where the tendons of the neck meet jawbone. Drawn by desire, by
    resonance of touch. I think of snow

drifts and riding my bike into stinging rain as it turns to sleet—after I've
    tossed the last paper in a perfect, parabolic arc over the last hedge, so
    Ronnie Reagan's weathered face smacks like a palm
against an empty box, against the last door of the last colonial on the
    corner of Mitchell and Main, and then picking up speed on slippery
    streets, gliding, sliding my ten-speed toward the lights of a home that
    after all this time
delivering the news, feels more like memory than a place where a wood
    burning stove waits, wanting to pulse and throb like a heart in a
    basement where I'd strip down, peeling off the damp cold clothes.
    There,

in the house, before my parents and sisters made it home from practices
    and lessons and jobs and errands, in the shelter
of the suburbs, in the time of the last plague
when we all still loved the Cardinal, trusted our priests, and rap was
    something we listened to
only on headphones, and fear was existential and far off as a comet
    hurtling toward earth, or a shuttle enveloped in a fiery plume. How
    we protected ourselves

from ourselves until the chill reached bone. Naked, alone, I would feed
the fire, log upon log, sticks, old newspapers, until it built to a blaze
and roared like the engine of a steam locomotive, and the gauge on the
stovepipe pushed yellow to orange and far into dangerous red,
a zone where heat blossomed, bloomed until even the family dog would
lift herself from sleep and slowly creep away. And I'd stand there until
I glistened

in a sheen of sweat. *You run hot*, you say, *like a furnace*—fanning your cool
palm against my chest, and I think of that boy who could never seem
to get warm enough. Blazing past snowdrifts that melt in my wake,
the sleet turning back to rain before it hits my face, then steaming off,
hissing, ice melting beneath

the wheels, and all the trees burst into flower. I am gathering speed. I am raising
the dead—delivering the news to everyone, and for once it really is
Morning in America, and even old Ronnie, benign in neglect, feels a
stirring of love, of rage, of righteousness, of the fear that comes not
of each other but from never being known: the fear of fear and being
alone and cold so cold that no fire could touch us, reach us, could ever
make us warm.

The Quantum Soul

And I think of how, as a boy, at a greasy summer fair in Maine, I cranked
    the handle of the ancient Mutoscope and watched the pictures flip
    and blur to life—a woman dancing naked on a stage with two huge
    feather fans and how
for months I could not watch a film without trying to see into and through
those spaces. I'd stare so hard it hurt my head. And how my friend Pete's
    father wouldn't enter a room if the lights were fluorescent—*those*
    things mess with your brain he said *they don't glow they flicker, so fast you can't*
    see it. See it? That light
isn't on or off. That's why they buzz . . . *Listen.* And I didn't and I did. And
    they did with the flickering wings of a thousand insects. And I
    still don't like them. How they turn the magic to a trick, a game.
    Somewhere deep inside

inside the brain we are both on

and off and neither: and events are taking place, flickering and piling
    up beyond the speed of comprehension. And how I knew this kid
    who had these mini-seizures where he'd just shut off in the middle
    of a conversation or while we were tossing a ball so it would float on
    past a frozen glove or hit him smack
in the cheekbone, and we'd laugh when he came back, confused and
    bruised. We place a thing near another thing and it throws a spark,
    makes a third somehow in there and out, a process we name art (or
    God?). To wade knee-deep in the night-river and cup a handful of
    stars and try to drink them as they stream and shiver down your
    arms.   Our brains evolve (one word contains another word that
    means

entanglement) to learn the gap is not

a gap—it is a charge, a fire. Years later, Pete's dad was taken off in
handcuffs for selling kiddie porn from his basement. And someone
told me how that kid went through a stoplight at 50 miles an hour
and spent three days unconscious before he came awake. *And the
seizures*

were gone.

RE: Like a Box

This box is not a box, not a coffin, not a cell, not a window that wills and welcomes light into your home, casting a perfect square of sleep onto the floor. This knot is not a knot. It's come undone. Laces, trailing in the wind, catch in the chain-drive, flipping the rider up and over the handlebars (the first of many times I've flown apart). A product of forgetting all I thought I knew, all that I forgot. Unraveling, (unmasking, unmaking). Houdini in the water-tank struggling to release his ankles from the stocks, works his magic, unsnaps the locks. Once as a boy I watched in awe as a man crawled from the black smoke of a burning car, pulling his body through the window as if out of the deep water and onto the dock. Once as a boy I walked into an almost empty church and saw a woman's voice leave her throat in a flight of wings that became a flock of blackbirds wheeling, beating against the windows and the walls. And I have seen my sons turn a cardboard box into a submarine, an airplane, a spaceship. And I have seen one of them made to disappear into a box beneath the ground but somehow when I speak to him he's everywhere at once and uncontained, a rhythm sprung. This box is not a coffin. But what we would escape into and from—bodies transforming into wings and water and smoke. And if a poem is not salvation it might just be its metaphor: it does what a metaphor does: sheds its skin and slides away, getting at a thing by traveling out, making connections, growing larger as it goes until it can hardly contain itself, seeking itself in other lives, rhythms, bodies, gods: (How the solo can almost unmake the song). We say the great ones played "outside the box," and that night on the little square of a stage in France in 65 when hell and hope was breaking everywhere Coltrane channeled the divine, dove deep into himself, and took off in a run, was thrown, flung, gone, not gone: a new mathematics in fevered notes that shivered up against each other, the possible impossible: multiphonic sheets of sound, overtones, reaching up and up and up and up into an almost painful wail: the pilot having flown too far into the outer edges of the atmosphere grown dizzy, forgetting the passengers, the earth itself, and dragging us with him, ready or not. And my God the stars, the stars—some already gone a millennium but sending their light on anyway, knowing how long it can take a message to find us, having faith it must. Some dying. Some not yet born. And in being born again, this poem is not a coffin, not a cell, not a box full of dust any more than a flower is—or a fire or the light of a long-dead star, or any great love. This poem will not click shut.

Any Moonwalker Can Tell You II

To see the earth and the sun in the same sky at the same time is to reach
    up with a mason jar and ask the gods

to fill it with our own reflection. This is the eye behind the other eye,
    corneas expanding. This is the sky, a series

of lenses telescoping backward over the alps and craters and the planes
    and all the planets. To stand inside outside

on the highest hillside with all our faith and fragility—lights glowing on,
    and off, and on again, silent, fire-flying.

Preoccupied at a Café in Portland, Maine

For Rachael

Where are you now? you ask and I blink my way back from across traffic and
the other side of the a busy street where a man holds a small transistor
radio to his ear and bounce-walks ten steps one way and ten steps back
and I can't tell if he is singing along or having a conversation with some
distant civilization on some other dimensional plane *live via satellite*. I want
to say *I am always in so many places: here and gone. Everything*

intersections, interactions—the kid playing "Burning Love" on her guitar, the
coins shining in the velvety case, the way that song will follow us all home
for days—right now a part of me I've secreted away is sledding too fast
down a hill with our son holding on behind me and our dog chasing and
you shouting from the top of the hill, *look out*

for the boulder, so I laugh for what seems like no reason, with the world
around us all city and blackbirds and coffee and the summer ocean
misting across the bay. Which might explain

why you catch me grimacing and ask if I'm in pain *is it your hip or your
back?* and I don't know what to say. Maybe it's the resonance of pain, its
habit. How we are all in a state of continuous occupation,

like Eastern Europe, and even if the armies leave, even if the wall
comes down, we will build another wall in the absence of its memory.
Preoccupied, post-occupied. How we set our jaws and grind our teeth
for what has been and what comes. I want to say how exhilarated
and exhausted I feel when it comes together like this—the man, the
blackbirds, the coffee, the snow, Eastern Europe with all its tanks and
concrete and all those dimensions like a book dropped into a puddle, its
ink running, it pages stuck together. Once I believed

to be aware would be divinity, prophecy—to see clearly the unified field from the top of the mountain. Elvis in a baby-blue, rhinestoned jumpsuit—sweating and shining and stoned and everywhere at once, on a million TV screens. Where is the message

in a brand new language come falling like gravity through everything? *Where did you go just then? Where were you?* Like someone aflame and tearing off his clothes as he runs through winter, I am coming back to you, naked and singing.

Going Sideways

That's when it all went sideways, he says, leaning forward in the rain, drawing
deep on his cigarette and it's funny how many things you think in a
moment like that, like *who says that* and *what does it mean?* Like wheels
losing traction on a slick road and the truck sliding ass-first down an
embankment? Or how heat lightning splits across an August evening sky,

cloud-leaping? Or how my son, one night in a desert, flew through a
windshield, shattering into memory. Or more, the way everything
is always careening, the way someone told me once how the galaxy
is sliding, sideways across the universe at murderous speed and all I
could think was—*sideways? In relation to what, exactly?* But sideways we
are going and I've already lost the thread of my friend's story—
which seems very important to him. This life has a way of slipping

past our defenses. Sidling up, making its excuses, saying, *is this seat taken?*
and sitting before you can answer. A man stumbles off the curb
with a *Trump That Bitch* t-shirt riding halfway up his gut. I'm looking
while not looking, trying not to hope he gets hit by the truck with the
testicles hanging off the back. So much is a waiting for something
crazy to happen or a waiting for something to end. A wishing we
could slip the moment we inhabit for a new city a new state of being,
a brand new pair of pants.

Memory is like that, the mind refusing to stay where we are or go where
we are going. Most animals move in the direction they are facing.
Except for crabs (which move sideways) and the naked mole rat of
East Africa which has evolved

to move backwards rapidly. The man has started to spin in a circle while
drifting into the middle of the street. Somehow no one is hitting

him. Somehow no one even blows a horn in warning, recognition. I imagine he's a mole-rat in a *Trump That Bitch* t-shirt (I refuse to imagine him naked)

and laugh. And my friend says, *I know, right? It's funny.* And I say *yeah, sure is.* Because whatever it is he's talking about now, I'm sure it's hilarious when seen from the right perspective. *Can a naked mole-rat spin,* I wonder? And would it have this Neo-from-the-Matrix-like ability to avoid getting run over while careening diagonally across an intersection? And just like that, the mole-rat-man becomes a galaxy.

Or just another version of me. Another iteration. One that managed to avoid collisions. So much

is just the way we form connections. Trying to make sense of things. Astrocartography. Charting our minds among the stars while the world wheels and spins. As a chubby boy of twelve, padded and sweating through late summer football practices, I learned to keep my head on a swivel. It is important to pay attention. Not only to what's ahead but behind and to either side flashing in from the corner of the eye. I do not travel backwards

easily. I circle back in widening arcs

to the same songs, the same pictures floating from between the covers of the same books, the same unfinished arguments,

to the same desert highway under the same stars reflected on the same dead sea. And wherever I am, I am always drifting off to sleep and my oldest son is always sitting up front, his head silhouetted, a shadow unshattering. And the van is going seventy toward Aqaba as the driver's chin dips toward his chest. Beyond our seeing, miles ahead, a truck is parked across the road. And I can't do anything. We will keep going forward until it is too late to turn. We will plow straight ahead and in and maybe spin until we stop again. And I will spend the rest of my life asleep while waking, listening while not listening, trying to escape from where I am and where I've been and will keep going (because I don't know how to stop) wishing somewhere back there somehow it could have all gone

sideways.

II. In Case of Emergency

Arrhythmia

In memory everything seems to happen to music—Tennessee Williams

"Association" is not a luxury, but one of the very conditions and prerogatives of freedom—
Judith Butler

1.

There is a shyness and a wish in the song of tires on the interstate after
rain—a consoling shhh that settles like a hand on a shoulder or fingers
gliding through a child's hair or the soft roll of cymbals fading at the end
of the last torch ballad an hour past last call when everything is settling
toward silence still swelling and swollen with a promise it will come again.
It will come again, I say, whispering. It is almost rhythm almost pattern,
illusory and pregnant. A shifting space between that hesitates with all the
love and lust of a back-line drummer on Bourbon Street. I have never
been a man to rest in silences and sometimes I struggle to listen, to wait.
Too in love with my own voice shoving the silences away as if trying to
answer a question I was too afraid to ask my father my first girlfriend the
homeless man who flashed my first wife, Susan, at a bus-station in Omaha
in 1998. Or maybe I have always been asking just not waiting hurrying
away to the next appointment the next class, stepping onto the next bus,
away from the conversation, waving thoughts away through windows, half
wondering at the silent shapes those mouths have made.

2.

Yesterday while stepping into the office, a cry cut the air, making me stop and turn—my hand still reaching for the door, foot caught mid-step. Behind me, only the avenue churning with engines and students weaving through them, and one old, heavy woman in a long white coat pushing a wheeled chrome walking cage, and leaning into it as if against a strong wind. I thought, a crow maybe, or a child shouting through the backseat window, for no reason at all except for being that child in that car or maybe just to startle a preoccupied professor late for class. I almost turned again, then, *AIEEAAAAH*. Sharp and winged. The woman's head tilted up, her gray hair hanging straight and heavy as a model's emerging from blue water, her neck drawn lithe and taut. *AIEEAAAAH*. The note bending on a long string, wavering. Then everything shifting back into that lumbering glide as if nothing at all had happened as if *this happens all the time. It does.*

3.

For one year as a boy I'd wake up screaming or wake myself with my screaming or my father terrified, hair matted and wild with sleep, would grip a damp shoulder shaking me until I stopped screaming. Not every night. Sometimes five days apart, then ten, fifteen, then back to five again. And once, three nights running. It got so he couldn't fall asleep or would wake for no reason at all, wondering if he heard me in his dreams, wandering up the stairs to my room, listening. He doesn't remember any of this. I don't remember the dreams.

4.

I fear most, not the forgetting but how it vanishes—erased, released so we might better keep our grip on what and who we would believe we were and are, the way the mind replaces what we see and hear and sense— adding details, writing over thoughts until it is another thing entirely. When does the name of the child separate from the child, become the only child—only the child—the photograph replace the skin alive with heat. So much is story. Words replace the blinding blue of a winter sky, the actual steam release of air-brakes, bloom of breath, exhaust, and bitterness of cigarettes which is a taste a touch a sound embodied and the body, a refracted image, broken into wholeness.

5.

Reaching back each thought of my father begins with music—Oldies 103 and winter trees blurring past us on 128 and cold vinyl seats, his warm baritone released in puffs as the Cavalier's engine worked to warm us, its wipers scraping frost as the heater growled and pulsed and clear glass bloomed up from the dash in a bright blue inverse cloud melting at the edges as we crooned with Elvis and Sinatra, my father's voice blending into the mix, matching tone and pitch as if it had all been engineered and I'd come in high and piercing, off, voice crackling like wet saplings in a fire and it was all fire and flashing windshields all around.

6.

I do not know if my son screamed when the van struck the truck, when the glass shattered around him when he was, for an instant, thrown to flight. I was asleep in back, until I wasn't. I did not hear and can't stop hearing. I did not see and can't stop seeing. Screaming. Singing.

7.

Ten steps and a cry again. Then five. Then fifteen and everyone looking away or down at their feet as she made her way past the student center and the purring SUVs and the CVS on 20th street. And for the rest of the day I found myself listening and waiting, wondering if I listened hard enough, could I hear it somewhere back behind everything, behind the rumble of the air-conditioners and the chatter in the hallways and my lecture on Tennessee Williams and my voice speaking the words of Tennessee Williams which are too brutally beautiful to have ever been. And I wrote them on the white-boards and the chalk-boards waiting and staring at the spaces between them listening in everything I heard and almost heard for the cry. In silence that isn't really—is only a hesitation under white-noise that's really just a blurring of a thousand pistons firing—a thousand small explosions blazing fast and indistinct. And is all of us and is always happening.

8.

And maybe it is all the same—same song, same cry, sung or would be if we could be listeners reaching down to the root of it—articulate—a shuddering with longing and maybe it is not our work to remember this and maybe the actual is ephemeral and maybe that's its beauty and ours is a different thing —the getting close while drifting back—the almost wavelike reaching of the sea and maybe the best that we can say is yesterday I heard this cry and I thought of my son and it was like and it was like and it was like and it was like and it was like and it was like and it was like and it was

a bird bursting out of shards of light refracting stars over a desert into story into memory transformed, shapeless, shapely, taking on the body and ballast, the ballet of a boy thrown free of his body.

This is what listening means—finding in the storm, the harmony, the single tap of rain among the many rhythms, the molecule of hydrogen in silence beating like a heart among so many which is to find the unheard unuttered cry of one's own child in the eyes of a girl staring from a broken city, in a woman's unhinged wailing, in the body washed up on the beach a world away as the waves pound sand to sand drawn to and from the sea.

Field Sobriety

It is near the close of summer days as the earth cools toward evening and
    the first chill of autumn tap
taps at my window like a local cop with the butt-end of his flashlight, to
    wake the sleeping driver parked at the edge
of a starry field, cracking open his dreams:

Sir, I'm sorry but you can't sleep here. Are you Ok? Have you had anything to
    drink? and I am startled and confused by the light and the dark
and the light again, waiting for my eyes to make
sense of things, to send a message to my brain

that can process *Do you know where you are? Can you step out of the car please?*
    As I reach
for my wallet *Keep your hands where I can see them.* And my
registration. I am coming back
to myself but I can't quite recognize

the destination as if I've wandered into a room and forgotten
the reason and look helplessly up to the backlit shape of a voice caught
somewhere between
concern and a low rumble of anticipation. I know
how little I am known, how potentially dangerous

each moment is. How much even a simple misunderstanding can cost.
    How hard it can be to stand
on one leg and recite the alphabet backwards, as if the roots of language
    could take me back

to the beginnings of things, counting down to liftoff. Because the truth is I have been

driving under many influences for many years. Sometimes all it takes is
   a single hawk flying low along a field at sunset and I forget myself
   and follow it

for miles. And always I am pulling off the road to places I shouldn't be,
   singing out

with the windows down or drinking in a field of stars, tipped to my lips
   by the wind and I am

probably up to something—though I've lost sight

of what it is and don't much care. And if you were to search

the car, you'd find contraband somewhere, something even I have not
   discovered yet, or thought about—

something hidden beneath the seat or underneath the spare. I hope

there is some trouble there and that you find it.

A Word Misheard

—There is a wideness to God's mercy

There is a wildness to god's mercy, like the wildness of the sea I thought I heard
her sing—that swinging bell of a woman at the steps of the chancel,
belting out the hymn. As I imagine even God mishears the echoes
in old churches, synagogues and temples, there being so many, their
sounds overlapping, their prayers incessant. It must be

like listening to a thousand radio broadcasts at once heard as one random
signal, at equal intensity at different frequencies. Constant power
spectral density. In the way that we mishear the sounds of the ocean
and its many bird-cries, many groans as rhythmic rolling anapests
advancing, receding at the edges

of this wide wild country that seems always to be tearing at itself and
screaming like a man removing his watch, his wedding ring, leaving
his phone on the seat of the bus to take off at a run and dive into the
crowded city as if it were a wave. Or the neighbor who hammered
nails into the basement door and shouted—*stay away*

from me. How long did I hum the melody with my eyes shut like a chorus
boy while she sung and swung high above, arms tiring with nowhere
to fall, ringing an alarm that started somewhere intimate and broke
apart over Beacon St. in a shower of warm rain or mist rising from
stone? We sing along as if we are alone, wishing we were free

of the refrain, of each other, of the world inside a verse, ourselves in
the world, a word, awhirl. Perhaps there is a mercy in words misheard
as many encounters with many wild birds becoming one bird flying
over a wide wild sea.

New and Bitter Flowers

We begin with the corpse of the deer in the road on the way to Loews to
buy new and bitter flowers and herbs for the garden we had planted
the evening before only to wake with our morning coffee to stems of
tulips and violas and the ruined azalea chewed down to its bones—
red and pink petals sprayed everywhere. *It looks like a bomb went off
in here*, Rachael said, as if she'd just entered our son's room on a
Saturday. *Damned deer!*

Which is to begin with two endings of two different stories that seem
like the same story because I can't see this deer without imagining
him, alive and elegant and with one or two others guided by the moon
and the scent of blossom into the sub-tropic warmth of our yard in
summer, to chew on flowers as we slept. And I wish I could have seen
it. And wish I could get the image out of my head. We can't

feel everything, can we? And sometimes aren't we blessed by what we
don't have to see? Imagine being so raw that each of our unnumbered
dead shook us by the shoulders, saying *wake up, wake up*. So raw that
deer driven by hunger into the human world dipping their heads only
a few feet away from our beds to feast would enter our sleep and tear
it apart with their little teeth. So raw

that we had to think about each time we almost didn't make it to where
we were going, how close we have come to being clipped by the semi
to be lifted and spun, toppling over and over like a doll dropped
from the window of a car by a child. Would we ever leave the safety
of our rooms? Would we ever enter them and risk closing the doors
behind us? Could we even sleep? It is too much

for any of us. And so we plant marigolds and vincas, basil and rosemary throughout the garden as if from them we might weave a dreamcatcher to fasten to the wall above a child's bed, as if dreams could be caught or warned away or watched from safe distances. As if we were not all driven to the same places by the same hungers. Or that we don't ache to wake one night among the dear, awash in the moon, our mouths full of flowers.

Witness

The ball I threw while playing in the park / Has not yet reached the ground—Dylan Thomas

Once

from the edges of a pond out by the bogs, I watched a dog break
through the ice. A big brown beast
of a mutt, chasing a yellow ball, had sprinted out too fast, too far, to where
the frosted white had gone to grey and black with shimmering. I
    remember how my own short breath
puffed clouds into a blinding chill that did not blind enough—a child
    trying to forget before the happening as if
you could unsee unhear unreal a thing, that you saw coming or if I
    turned and pedaled hard enough away or even closed my eyes, the
    ball would stop
mid-air, reverse its flight
or disappear, and maybe I would not be there, having never taken the
    shortcut home from Pete's house through the woods
and never seen that dog, that ball. And somehow knowing even then
    how everything once touched must carry a scar. And we can't help
but be touched. He yelped and spun to splash in frozen sun—a ball
    locked in his jaws, and reached and reached again for edges
that splintered with his boy's laugh rising to a scream—brittle and
    blinding behind and out in front and everywhere

at once.

RE: Wisdom

You think wisdom is a passive thing—that you can sit by idly, pretend
    that sleep is listening. So you shelter
in place, knowing you are not the target. There must be a place between

meeting rage with rage and not giving a shit, between living in fear and
    ignoring the threat.

Wind and breaking waves push water toward the beach and parents
    whisper, *watch the kids*, knowing how a current forms a rip, knowing
how quickly calm can turn and pull even the best of swimmers beyond
    reach. The line between floating
and drowning is thin and may be in knowing how to resist

in what direction
and when. To swim
directly at the current or along
the beach. Or stay out of the water. Always

there is a mother tearing her hair and screaming for the lost and the ones
    who might be saved—who knows her children are everywhere, a
    voice gone ragged, warning if one

is in danger, they are all, and so are we. *Stop.*
You're scaring the kids, someone says even as the river of foam forms on
    the surface and the water muddies.

Even as the shore recedes.

In Case of Emergency
—For Rachael, November 9 2016

It's almost as if we were waiting for this, for someone to wake us, shake
us, saying, *ALL THE ALARMS ARE GOING OFF. THE GLASS
IS BROKEN.*

The gloved fingers of the stage magician slip along the assistant's
abdomen, her long white ribbon of an arm flung toward the audience
(a trick of light on a swiftly moving river). Distraction, misdirection
as we shift and shuffle our cards, so lost in our craft we miss

the look that lingers from across the aisle and slides away, the look that
says *you aren't fooling anyone. I see what you're doing. I see everything.* Maybe
there is no depth, no point. Nothing (up my sleeve) but surfaces:
right now

a siren weaves through the city as the rain comes diving toward pavement
as a woman in a white dress runs across the street against the light as
the sun breaks through a cloud as the road begins to roar and steam
as cotton clings to hips as leaves torn from the branches explode in a
flock of starlings. When everything is always at my earlobe breathing
heavy and hot with lungs as full as any long distance runner's, wild-
ness is just another kind of intricacy,

an intimacy of layering one upon another and another: not one clock
but thousands—all ticking, all chiming. Running down and winding
up. Once, driving with the windows down on interstate 93 through
Boston in the middle of summer I swallowed up the wet heat of the
stars and all the streetlights, headlights, floodlights steaming from the
harbor and sang them back. It sounded like Roy Orbison—smooth

on the tongue, sexy with longing but fragile in the way that skin after love can tremble like the surface of a pond near a highway—the birdwing flutter of 600,000 hearts.

Why do we resist each other? Insist on controlling each breath, lining up the shot. Why work so hard against the body that grunts and sweats its desire to connect? Seducing. Demanding. When the only secret left is

I've never invented anything. I put things together to wrench things apart. And I've never told anyone this, but once, broken on the side of a road in a desert I felt something in me crack and something being pulled through like air into a vacuum or like a child caught in an undertow. (But I was on the shore watching and I was the child. I was ocean). Last night

while we were making love, I came undone. Each bone unhinged, unlocked, each cell scattering with urge and ache. To rush back alight, awake, a warning *that it will all be lost if only so we have to search for it again: that to be human is not a failing*, but a falling from great height through leaves and branches, shifting light. Too bright. Fulgent. A fly unzipped. An embarrassment

of riches, a falling apart that might be the sound of shattering or another kind of opening, that space we make and in making still might reach across.

Sewers

1.

In the alleyway behind the one convenience store on 18th Street beneath a sign that claims the *coldest beer in town*: a boy squats, spidery, tossing stones into a sewer drain, listening for echoes or the sound of water, or some keening call. There are currents in the nights, beyond the porchlight where I've seen the bright eyes bobbing into darknesses, vanishing beneath the street. Once I watched a doll ripped from its owner then kicked past her clawing hands into the gutter and away. We lose things down there, that way—rubber balls, coins, the sound of cruel laughter and of wailing, that part of us that thought to help, step in against the bigger, sharp-boned boys, and try with wild swings that would have failed to strike at anything except for air—for me at 48, waking, rubbing the jaw unbruised, eyes unswollen, the long straight slope of cartilage. An image of a skinny girl in a flowered dress, bunched above her boyish hips. Her arm has gone has disappeared into the drain, fingers splayed out reaching into space. I have been told how nothing is lost, that everything that flows away returns. Somehow. It does. Just not the way we'd hope.

2.

Here the floods come sudden come fierce, not the filling of a bowl, or a promise, or overflow of bathwater lipping over porcelain to soak the floor and fill the basement, drip by drip. No. All along Hal Greer Boulevard, water geysers up and out, open throated to a world we've learned is only skim, a film across the top of some great sunken sea. And now it is risen. It is risen indeed. With all the force of answering each voice ever raised in supplication, in song, in prayer, in rage, in fear to force a 40 pound manhole cover spinning into air: up and off and down the street. On 5th and 6th, and 14th, sewer lines collapse, pavement giving way, crumbling in to sinkholes, catacombs, water rising to crest and seek the depths again, to bring each holler to one level, one depth, a flattening, and streets are rivers rushing into ponds of parking lots. And underpasses fill beneath a railroad line that splits the city, stranding trucks and SUV's, taillights red and blinking, blinking helplessly.

3.

Sometimes I imagine them the way my students must see poems, dark
and depthless, dangerous with hidden things, their tunnels snaking
aimless as forever out beneath the city under rivers north and south and
thick with mysteries: the giant alligators of New York, that clown of
Stephen King's, spiders, rats the size of dogs, the bones of Jimmy Hoffa,
Jesus, Weldon Kees doing the backstroke through churning rivers of
waste, projecting downward things we've lost or buried or hidden from
ourselves (which might be words for the same thing in the way that words
are always a way of seeing not seeing). Hugo said of Paris that the city
has another city underneath, like some dark mirror full of blind alleys,
crossroads, stench. And looking down into these holes that swallow men
we cannot help but feel the pull to know to see ourselves or lose them
(which might be words for the same thing in the way that words are
always pulling with the current of an impure stream) and maybe starve
or fill our pockets with the treasures of the careless and the dead or
wrestle with some mythic beast fed massive with our hunger, then come
back slick, brown with its defeat, bright-eyed beaming—a prophet of
shadows and of stink, of sewers (which might be poems or one great
poem that shifts and churns beneath, in the way that words form tunnels
wet with echoing).

Suffering Tape

We have the tape. I don't want to hear the tape. No reason for me to hear the tape . . . because it's a suffering tape. It's a terrible tape. I've been fully briefed on it. There's no reason for me to hear it.—45

Sometimes I think I am haunted most by what I haven't heard. What is
   caught in the throat almost inaudible. Drowned out. Cut off. Mid

sentence. Pieced

apart and tossed away. Ignored. Sounds that are lost, like the voice of
   my oldest son on his 7th birthday. I know there is a tape of him
   singing somewhere but I haven't heard it. Don't want to.

As a boy I learned to sing by matching sounds—Sam, Aretha, Marvin,
   Otis, James Brown—reaching from the dashboard down into my
   chest until I hollered with them and the windows of the Chevy
   steamed. Dizzy, I could see myself spool out to blues and reds with
   golds of early evening sun and shadow as I shook and took the
   shape of starlings flocked or the flame of sunfish staring up at night
   from the windshield's blue-black pond, and dart off into fields of
   stars: that was long before I heard the chains rattling behind the
   chorus, long before

I learned what breaking meant, how it was transformation; it was
   crackling; it was resonant. How if you listen close/in/hard/far
   enough, if you stilled your breath, your beating blood, somewhere
   behind the chatter and the noise there would always be a keening,
   always be a song. To be in rhythm is an act

of listening—to find the space between the blows, where we fit and
    where we don't and how to move and when
In a room somewhere

in the back of the consulate, the air conditioning purrs and swells then
    pulls back in upon itself as someone loops a cry, drops a beat (anything
    can be a drum, especially the body: the belly, the chest, the back of the
    skull). The quickened panting, *gasping* . . . and the fists keep

hammering. A crack of something precious, irreplaceable and soft. *I can't*
    breathe, I can't breathe. A scream. *Put your earphones in or listen to the music,*
    like me. Then the sound of listening

to ourselves. Where silence is made

of a hundred thousand choirs, a chorus of chainsaws. The hiss of a
    cassette. The groove running down. Static. Wind. An ocean.

We choose what we listen for and what we don't. Our record might just be

the damage we have done, debris

on the floor among the glass as the jets fly off—or

a cry thrown out of the body, into song.

The Tongue is a Fire

How great a forest is set ablaze by a small fire! And the tongue is a fire.— James 3:5

Leaping from dry branch to dry branch, they come, feral things, desperate
    in their need to not just represent, but be. Imagine the word for
    lightning as it strikes. Words

I've loved too much and often without discretion, the way people love
    their nasty little children. You know the ones, running through the
    pews at the wedding, giggling, their ties and ribbons come undone,
    trailing behind them like contrails or the tails of kites in wind, as
    hard to chase down as a rumor. And I have always been that child
    left alone with a lighter in the sewing room, a basketful of remnants
    at his feet. Dangerous

at parties and worse at a faculty meeting. My father used to say, never
    miss an opportunity to keep your mouth shut. Which is to say, I
    have made a life of missed opportunities. The pleasure and pressure
    of silence is to smolder. To hold off is to withhold: pulp breaking
    down, gas rising as smoke and then the blossom in the chest. A new
    sun contained in being born. To be silenced is to be locked inside
    yourself, leashed beneath the hand that holds the whip, pausing at
    the edge of release. Coming to lips

like lips to a lover. Always that young, always learning and yearning as
    if it were the first time first taste: that heat in the mouth as the
    mouth opens and exhales and the pulse along the neck below the
    jaw begins to throb. Then the first tentative flicks and the promise of
    more. All thoughts are afterthoughts to those who use words to find
    out what they know. As in the dark, we see with hands, with tongue,
    relearning the body's curves.

It's breathy glottal fricative. The uvular n's and m's. A retroflex
articulation with its come-hither, right-swishing tail. I am a word
voyeur, an omnivore, a connoisseur. You watch my mouth. I'll watch
yours. Each overheard conversation in the coffee shop a symphony,
each argument a feast. Some nights I can barely rest

for all the chirrups and chewing in a world of heartbeats. Rachael moans
a doorway to a dream and silently I enter, head bowed in her cathedral.
In the morning she tells me that I talked in my sleep. But she can't
repeat what I've been saying, and I want to know the language

for regret and prayer and sorrow, tugging at the sleeves of my coat,
saying, *Don't pretend that you don't know me.* I try to pull away and they
follow shouting my name in echoes down the alleyways of debts and
promises. Silence can be made of sounds

that we won't own, or say out loud: *Don't you know the cost? Can't you hear
yourself? You don't listen. Understand. Sometimes I think. You selfish.
Ungrateful. Insensitive*

and take the shape of shame. And so, even when there is no one to
hear me, I whisper to myself, composing, trying out each combination,
searching for

a different kind of spell, to push open the door and flood the room with
oxygen. Where I am left

sifting through the ashes, covered in soot, saying *sorry I'm so sorry* even
as we burn.

What It Means to Drift

apart, to be a body as it slips away as if we were a mere suggestion of a
    gesture, a slow forming wave

goodbye or the promise of a swell that never crests. An old friend says
    the man I knew died in the accident. I think, at bottom

we are all bass, all rhythm or rhythms, high notes flashing on the surface
    of the sea, ranging, rearranging, in any order any shape we can
    imagine as long as we remain

in time, in key. Someone suggests a phrase and that becomes a theme
    and then we play with it, build on that, going where it leads, and in
    the building make and take

away, erasing as we add and add again until we've made

a brand "new" thing. The way that practiced fingers feel along the body's
    strings, to find new combinations, notes to build and build until
    the muscles ripple down the belly, coalescing into shudder, moan,
    ululation, scream. It is a wonder

this becoming

and going and how it all takes on such weight. *The man I knew*

died in the accident. Thank God. New skin, new scars. Everything dying
    and being

born again—the big blue notes of misremembering. Mis

understanding our way to sense. Yesterday

my father kept repeating the same story as if in the telling he might make
it stop

slipping away. I didn't say *you told me this already* or wish for who he was
(who should be a memory?). But watched him search

the way skilled hands reach for a melody remembered from a dream.
And find himself and lose himself. Somewhere, way down

the beach I heard a cry flung to the sea. It is a wonder how a sound can
travel, becoming its momentum thickening, deepening, until it is its
after-image. Sometimes

we have to see past all the echoes of what the gulls of evening scream.
Sometimes I have to force myself to taste the salt-sting on the breeze.
Until the sky above the bay is alive with singing, until I remember

that I've never seen this ocean and never will again. Always new, always
changing. And my father

is saying *son? Are you still there? Are you still listening?* And far beneath us I
can feel the world begin to heave, sand slip over sand.

Yes. I'm here. Right here. As you never were, we are. I am.

Bone Music

At the street market in Stary Arbat under the shadow
of the Kremlin if you look hard enough and maybe listen you still can find
bone music, jazz on bones, ribs—Ella and Elvis, Bill Haley and his
 Comets, Chuck Berry and the Bopper, illegal, forbidden, grooved
 onto thin plastic
"discs," dug by teenage soviets from dumpsters behind
the concrete clinics, phosphorescent with images of skulls and spines,
 the wrists broken and bent, halted in ghostly
bloom, in process of being set, of reconnect the way bones do, all on
 their own reaching for bone, reaching to make you
whole. Make you reformed because the body remembers the break
the way a record records not just the instruments but the dust and the
 scuff and the scratch—all the manner
and madness of its making. And I can tell you healing is always a miracle
of the everyday: stem cells coalescing forming cartilage
forming tissue make a callus forming bone until in time you'd almost
 never know except for the ache
that comes on in the cold saying, *hello there, hello?* like voices come from
 the end of a hallway
made of stone. Or like Aretha singing from the bottom of the well.
 Aretha's ghost
troubling the waters. I have a nephew who hears through bone
conduction, a cochlear implant pressed to his skull, which makes me
 think of Beethoven biting down on a rod attached
to his piano so his skull
became a concert hall. Which makes me think of
the many hours I lay in a hospital bed looking at the x-rays
of my shattered hip and the fiery brightness of the pins and screws
and white-hot wires and the clouds of tissue forming around them

which seemed to be whispering to me somehow, of choices, and
    accidents, and
how in music an off-note, a mistake, can be embraced by the soloist and
    so become a part of the song. Something

new. Brother Bones what music would you make from this or would you
simply whistle long and low and shake your head in wonder. Or like the
    prophet
in the valley see a vision of them all rattling, reaching
for each other, growing sinew, and rising—as bones do. To unlock
the hips and swing and swivel in a cellar full of sweaty conspirators.

Yes, these bones can sing, set all my comrades dancing,
to a ghostly tune.

The Locomotive of the Lord

If the locomotive of the Lord runs us down, / we should give thanks that the end had magnitude—Jack Gilbert

1.

I have never lived so far from the tracks I could not hear a train, its whistle and chug washing over me like dawn across an ocean or a prairie, if light could grow loud as it came on, or you could feel it rising in your feet, swelling in your chest, as if the train had started somewhere inside you as something small and far away and was growing closer, growing larger, so you want to dive out of the way, but you can't

dive away from yourself—it is always

too late. The mother pulls her child back from the tracks—even though he is already 10 feet away—her breath warm against his face, her lips close to his ear, saying *no honey, this is not the one, this is not our train* and his eyes widen in wonder at the sheer momentum, the speed and force of it, the flash of metal, its windows blurring into a single sheath of all the tones of silver and the rushing sound and the bell ringing the end of the world and the feel of those fingers on his shoulders tightening their grip, digging in, knowing how the train is not only the train but the space

it makes, the pressure wave, how it goes through you, and goes on, pulling you by the belt of your coat, lifting, longing to follow after it, so you must lean against/into its wind, then leaving you behind, unbalanced and dizzy in the settling of leaves and dust and longing, the gentle sadness and surprise that we are still here, that it has faded, that wherever it is going it is gone and you can't chase it, and whatever and whoever it carries away, it is not you and yet you feel a part of you is going with it, the long string of your breath maybe, or a scrap of wonder that wonders if perhaps that was, in fact, your train.

Someone told me once, all metaphor is

2.

a proof for how the world connects or tries to. So, even the saddest darkest angriest poem is an act of love, an act of joy, lovemaking, being full of, being packed with, things, the stuff of life reaching for itself and for others, each thing getting as close at it can to the other things and throwing sparks. Dreaming of entering each other bodily then pulling away, sated and unsated. The sheets tangled around their feet. Maybe they tease each other about who will sleep in the wet spot. Maybe they spoon. Maybe they sleep. And on waking, reach for each other again.

I think

3.

of transfers and connections and tracks going everywhere, strong cables coupling cable-cars, coupling towns to cities, clasping the country together. As a boy I would walk down to the tracks with my best friend and we'd put pennies on the rails, then wait. Placing our palms to steel to feel the first vibrations in our hands as if the train could ride our nerves, our veins, as if in feeling it miles away we were connected, boy to rail to train. As if we were the train. Then scrambling up the embankment, then the explosion, the roar of wheels and wind. I do not know what happened to those pennies, flat and curved, the fingernails of some bronze god, but I remember their smooth heat, alive in my hands.

And if I were to rise

4.

from this chair and wander like a desert saint, down the stairs and out
of the house, barefoot, bareheaded, onto the damp road alive with stars,
leaving behind this desk and this laptop and coffee mug, and the 1099s
and W2s and the poetry book and guitar in the corner, impatiently leaning
against the wall—like some teenager, bored and nervous—waiting for a
pair of hands to press the strings and make them sing. If I were to get
up mid-

line, and walk out through the woods down to the holler where the tracks
are alive with the 765 rattling and steaming from Huntington toward
Hurricane and step onto the ties, arms outstretched, legs apart in front
of that train, to catch it and let it take me in one bright flash and the
screaming of brakes

I can't help but wonder at the ways we seek that brightness, desperate for
contact, grappling with the angels as they moan and scratch our backs
and bite down on our shoulder-blades, at how we tear down roads too
fast, and dive

off of cliffs, and out of planes, taking the needle or the pipe or the
pill, holding the smoke in our lungs as long as we can, falling into beds
and out of them again, coupling to uncouple, and if we're lucky, walk
away knowing you never really walk away which is, I think, a trying to
unhitch, to interrupt the signal, the hive-like buzz, by going through a
thing, feeling it completely and emerging, shaking off the salt and sea
and drying in the wind and sun's heat, cleansed. To live for an instant, in
the instant, with no expectations or regret. Someone else

will read that book, pay those taxes. The guitar will be sold at the church
yard sale to another skinny boy with long fingers and a head full of
music who will play it better than you ever could with your heavy, brick-

layer's hands. And it is a relief to know the world does not need us. That it might be better off, in fact. Have you ever seen a house off the road, overgrown with kudzu, so the edges are rounded and green and the shape of a house is only a suggestion, discernable from a distance? Have you ever wanted to part the leaves and enter it, hot and dark like a lung? Loss can be a deepening too, the maker of poems and songs written by your wife or son and much better than yours with all their angry love and abandonment.

I know too much

5.

about this, I think. And nothing. I know it is a privilege

to be restless and dream of throwing a perfectly good life away. And I'm
not going to. I am only saying

there is something about standing too close to the tracks as the ground
begins to shake and the urge that it creates that reminds me

of good bourbon which reminds me of good sex and good poems which
contain all the colors and flavors of sweat and risk (and the metaphors
too) which makes you

want to dive into them. In front of them. Which is to say, there is
something about the sound of a train.

After the accident

6.

when I was still relearning how to walk (there is so much I should explain) and couldn't drive and needed crutches to stand, and I swayed and ached with every tug and wobble of the world and was always in pain and Darius was little, only four. We rode the Amtrak from White River Junction down to Newark to visit Susan's parents, rumbling through the green-gray hills of Western Mass into Springfield through the chill concrete of mid-December. I had to get up early from my seat each time we had to change a train and it was cold in the vestibule between the cars and everything creaked and shook and rattled and the walls and floors shifted and vibrated. And it was hard to balance, so Darius kept tightening his grip around my leg. And the ticket agent came to check on us, *Sir? Are you ok?* And I said yes because what else could I say (there is so much I could explain). And I remember never wanting to reach that station, get off that train, but to stand there in the iron cage and ache with my boy's death-grip on a shattered hip, wanting to tell him to hold on with all his fear and strength and never let go. And I remember how he looked up at me through his wild hair, shivering, and how his looking ran me down and ran me through. Sometimes I don't know if grief may be love's measure or maybe just a part of this, that unrelenting pressure on a healing break, a muscle trying to reknit itself as the cosmos shakes.

There is so much

7.

I can't explain—anymore than I can translate the language of a mountain, its trees ablaze with wings, how love like pain like hunger makes us strangers to ourselves, and makes us do strange things: steal and plead, and suffer, and dance like David to the trumpets in the street, sharpening our senses as we lose our sense, making visions come, so I wake in the night, certain I am still in the house in Georgia with the yard full of chiggers and the chain-link fence where kudzu grows and creeps and the railroad tracks behind it are always on the verge of humming and trembling into life so that all the china rattles in the cabinet and Susan shifts and groans, her long black hair spread on the sheets like a downed raven's wing spread across a highway. I have heard the voice of the son I lost so many times and have risen from the bed and tried to find his room only to stop and stare about in disbelief at who and where I was and then slide down the wall, shaking, grateful, sick in the gut, sweating, chilled. This life is a beautiful

accident made of accidents we try to shape. And sometimes the sound of your son in the night is the distant whistle of a train rolling away.

After the honeymoon Rachael and I rode the Wolverine from Chicago

8.

back to Kalamazoo. It snowed through the service at St. Marks in Coldwater, through the reception, and the wedding night, and breakfast at her parent's farm, and the three days in the city spent mostly in hotel rooms. Glass boxes within boxes stacked on boxes, hovering over other boxes. All of them shining with their own light and heat and lights of the city. Warm spaces floating in the freezing air. Like stars among stars. If stars were packed close as they seem from a distance. Instead of millions of miles and years way. Separated by freezing space. How do I explain?.

Do you ever think of her when you are making love to me?

and I said no (it's like an ache, this ache at my hip maybe; she is there but over there and still inside of me and all around but not). You can make love in grief, in pain. You can dance to the Lord in a crowd and still be dancing as if they were not there, as if He weren't watching, as if She were watching (we do it all the time) make love in a box of warm air in a building full of other boxes other people, clicking through the channels, showering, making their plans for dinner, dressing for the show, undressing for each other, teasingly, slow, or quick and desperate. I think of Susan. I think of Cyrus in the way you think of deer on a hillside outside a bedroom, throwing on the floodlights as you sleep. You know that they are there and sometimes you would wish to run a hand across a back, feel their bones and heat, their hunger but you can't and sometimes you wake and stare and lock eyes for a minute and then they run off, run away.

And so

9.

we drank champagne we smuggled in a coat as the train plowed through
two feet of powder on a clear blue day and the snow exploded and
whirled around us, caught in the wind that the train had made

around the train, glittering in brilliant constellations, a comet entering
the atmosphere. A tunnel of sunlight, starlight, and frost wheeling and
dancing in space

I have been thrown onto the tracks and run through, felt the blast of
it, the heat and shudder, and have risen to find myself in disbelief,
uncoupled,

bones reaching for each other for themselves, only to be run down again
and that is how it is, for most of us I think. Unless

you are lucky and find yourself one day shivering, someone whispering
this is the one. This is us, our train and then maybe you step off the platform
and step up onto the stairs and find your seat. And you think, I will ride
this wherever it takes and be thankful. Thankful for the hand in your
hand and the blazing world outside your window picking up speed as it
goes, losing its shape, becoming a wash of white and green and blue and
gray. Thankful

for the city and the buried fields of wheat and corn. Thankful

for the son you've lost in a shower of sparks and the son waiting for you
at the farm and how sometimes you find one in the other. How one hand
becomes another, sometimes painful in their transformations, and how
they slip from your grasp. Thankful

for the grinding ache that reminds you of who you were and are. Thankful for the fleeting moments when you forget it's there. Thankful

for how it returns each morning as you rise from bed. Thankful for the impact and the magnitude

even as you hurtle toward your destination, knowing that you must

get off this train. Knowing you will

be run down and through

again.

JOEL PECKHAM, an Assistant Professor of English at Marshall University, is a poet, essayist and scholar of American literature who has published seven collections of poetry and prose, most recently GOD'S BICYCLE (futurecycle) and BODY MEMORY (New Rivers). He is also co-editor of the forthcoming anthology, WILD GODS: THE ECSTATIC IN CONTEMPORARY POETRY AND PROSE (New Rivers). His poems and essays have appeared in many journals, including *Brevity, Cave Wall, the North American Review, Prairie Schooner, Rattle, River Teeth, The Southern Review,* and *The Sun*. He lives with his family, Rachael Peckham and Darius Atefat-Peckham, in Huntington, WV.